BOLDNESS IN CHRIST

BY
JOAN E. MURRAY

Published by:
Intermedia Publishing Group Inc.
PO Box 2825
Peoria, AZ 85380
www.intermediapub.com

ISBN 978-1-935529-51-4

Printed in the United States of America

Scripture quotes are taken from the King James Version, New International Version, and Holman Christian Standard Bibles.

Cover Design by: Gabriela Garza and Robert Sugawa

TABLE OF CONTENTS

1 | WHAT IS BOLDNESS?

For God hath not given us the spirit of fear; but of power, and of love, and of a sound mind.

2 Timothy 1:7 (KJV)

Have you ever met anyone or do you know someone who is bold? What did you notice about that person? Did they seem fearless? Did they appear strong and invincible? We all experience times when we are required to be bold. Some of you have spoken up in the midst of unjust situations, yet others have allowed situations to intimidate and keep them from taking a stand for what is right. We are all required to operate in boldness in various seasons of our lives. When the opportunity comes, we must keep in mind that when we speak up for what is right, God is glorified.

As we shrink back and are fearful, we give the enemy a foothold in our lives to bring intimidation, fear, and worry to our hearts. Boldness is defined as being daring, brave, courageous, audacious, and to be ready. Boldness requires that we trample fear under our feet so we can be overcomers.

The scripture says that fear is a spirit and this spirit did not come from God. God is a God of faith and He has birthed children who are equipped with faith to do great things in life. When fear enters the picture, it causes us to create the worst possible scenario in our minds, which in turn causes us to shrink back from what God wants us to do. Fear causes us not to think clearly, but God has given us power to be victorious when this happens.

A few years ago, I experienced a situation on a previous job that could have caused fear to take root in my heart; but the Holy Spirit brought peace and wisdom about how I was to deal with the situation. The boldness of the Lord arose in my heart and I was able to stand firm and gain the victory. While at work, I inadvertently sent an e-mail I had received about Jesus to the wrong person. The person

WHAT IS BOLDNESS?

was offended and decided to pass it on to our boss. My immediate supervisor called to tell me about the problem right after he contacted her. She was concerned that this would affect my review and salary increase since she had just sent the yearly evaluations to him.

I called our boss and he was very aggravated with me for sending the e-mail through company e-mail. He was concerned that it could offend our clients and cause problems. I told him I had sent the e-mail to the person by mistake and apologized for the error; and I promised to be more careful about information I transmitted from my work e-mail. He continued to reiterate the problem and I boldly asked him if he had ever made a mistake. After a long pause, he calmed down and told me to be more careful.

I thanked him for his understanding; and, when my review and raise came through, they were not modified at all. Although the enemy wanted to use the situation to affect me in a negative way, God allowed His boldness to arise in my heart. It is the devil's job to intimidate and bully you into doing what he wants you to do, but God is fighting for you. I discovered that when you are genuinely sorry, and are willing to take responsibility for your mistakes, God will always vindicate you.

Do not allow the enemy to keep you from taking a bold stand for the things you believe. Do not let the fear of losing a job, relationship, or friendship, keep you in a cycle of always backing down and giving in. God will always back you and cover you! The Apostle Peter encountered times when fear tried to overcome him, and in some instances did overtake him for a season. Let us explore his story.

2 | PETER'S BOLDNESS

While Peter and John were speaking to the people, they were confronted by the priest, the captain of the Temple guard, and some of the Sadducees. These leaders were very disturbed that Peter and John were teaching the people that through Jesus there is a resurrection of the dead. They arrested them and, since it was already evening, put them in jail until morning. But many of the people who heard their message believed it, so the number of believers now totaled about 5,000 men, not counting the women and children. Then Peter filled with the

BOLDNESS IN CHRIST

Holy Spirit, said to them, "Rulers and elders of our people, are we being questioned today because we've done a good deed for a crippled man? Do you want to know how he was healed? Let me clearly state to all of you and to all the people of Israel that he was healed by the powerful name of Jesus Christ, the Nazarene, the man you crucified but whom God raised from the dead."

Acts 4:1-4, 8-11a (NLT)

In Acts chapter three Peter and John were on their way to the temple to pray; and, when they arrived they witnessed a man who was lame from birth being carried in. Each day someone would put the lame man down by the temple gate called Beautiful so he could beg for financial support.

When Peter and John were about to enter the temple, he asked them for some money. They stopped and told him they did not have silver and gold, but they would give him what they did have. They commanded him in the name of Jesus Christ, the Nazarene, to get up and walk. Peter then took the man by his hand and helped him up, and as he did the man's feet and ankles were instantly healed and strengthened. The man jumped up, stood on his own feet, and began to walk. Then, walking, leaping, and praising God, he went into the temple with them. This incident began a demonstration of the power of the Holy Spirit in the lives of Peter and John, but especially in Peter's life.

After the council witnessed this incident, they charged Peter and John and put them in jail until the next day. They had witnessed to thousands of people and many men and woman were won to Jesus. The council demanded to know by what power they were doing these things. Peter, filled with the power and boldness of the Holy Spirit, told them that it was Jesus -- God's Son whom they had crucified -- who healed the lame man. He reminded them that Jesus was the cornerstone whom God had sent to them but they rejected and then crucified Him.

BOLDNESS IN CHRIST

Their rejection had not stopped the plan of God -- Jesus was still the cornerstone. He boldly told them that salvation could not be found in any other name but Jesus. The council realized they had made a grave mistake because, as Peter and John defended themselves, they were continuing to witness about Jesus to those who were in the court. They tried to stop them, but they were unstoppable. These men were not well educated; but, because of the power of the Holy Spirit's presence in their lives, they were a marvel to behold. Even the council marveled at their knowledge and came to the conclusion that they were so knowledgeable because they had been with Jesus.

The power of the Holy Spirit, operating through their lives, gave them courage to stand boldly in their rightful authority. He has given you the same degree of boldness to stand in your God-given authority. He wants you to be as bold as a lion, as you share Jesus, and speak up for that which is right and true. As you and I operate in boldness, the Holy Spirit's power is displayed through us and He gives us victory in all situations.

3|BOLD FOR CHRIST

The members of the council were amazed when they saw the boldness of Peter and John, for they could see that they were ordinary men with no special training in the Scriptures. They also recognized them as the men who had been with Jesus. But since they could see the man who had been healed standing right there among them, there was nothing the council could say. So they ordered Peter and John out of the council chamber and conferred among themselves. "What should we do with these men?" they asked each other. "We can't deny that they have performed a miraculous sign, and everybody in Jerusalem knows about it. But to keep them from spreading their propaganda any further, we must warn them not to speak to any one in Jesus' name again." So they called the apostles back in and commanded them never to speak or teach in the name of Jesus. But Peter and John replied, "Do you think God wants us to obey you rather than Him? We cannot stop telling about everything we have seen and heard."

Acts 4:12-20 (NLT)

BOLD FOR CHRIST

Imagine being told not to speak the precious name of Jesus! I wonder what many of us would do if we were put in the situation of not being allowed to speak His name, knowing that we would either end up in prison or be killed if we did. With instructions from the council, the persecution of the apostles began to unfold.

When the council saw the man leaping, walking, and giving praise and thanks to God, they could not deny the evidence before their eyes. They also understood that this miracle could only have been performed because of Jesus, but they still refused to believe that He was God's Son. They had a problem, and they did not know how to solve it, so they plotted to shut the mouths of the disciples but could not stop the story. They discovered that the name and the power and authority of Jesus, coupled with the presence of the Holy Spirit, were unstoppable.

Peter and John's response demonstrated their deep love for Jesus, and their passion to see people healed, delivered, and set free by Him. They challenged the council about whether it was right in God's sight or theirs to listen to them rather than God, and the disciples boldly refused to obey them.

The boldness of Peter was remarkable because just a few weeks prior in the same place, and probably before the same people, he had denied Jesus three times. He had followed Jesus when He was arrested and taken before the council. Earlier that evening, Jesus had warned him that before the rooster crowed he would deny Him three times, and Peter had insisted that he would not.

During Jesus' trial and while Peter was sitting outside in the courtyard, a servant girl came over and said to him, "You were one of those with Jesus, the Galilean." But Peter denied it in front of everyone. "I don't know what you are talking about." Later that same evening another servant girl noticed him and said to those standing around, "This man was with Jesus of Nazareth." This time when Peter denied it he did so with an oath. Finally, a little later some of the other by-standers came over to Peter and said, 'You must be one of them, we can tell by your Galilean accent." Peter said to them "A curse on me, if I'm lying, I don't know the man!"

And immediately the rooster crowed. Suddenly, Jesus' words flashed through Peter's mind and he went out and wept bitterly (Matthew 26:69-75). It is interesting to note that the first two people who challenged Peter were two young women, and his denial occurred on the same night that Jesus was arrested. These young women probably had been in Jesus' meetings, witnessed His miracles or seen Peter walking, talking, and fellowshipping with Jesus.

While Jesus was being abused and tried before the council, Peter who had walked with Him, talked with

Him, broken bread together with Him, was just a short distance away denying that he ever knew Him. Peter loved Jesus, but fear overcame him. He distanced himself from Jesus because of fear that he would also be brought up on charges along with Him which kept him from defending Jesus.

After His crucifixion, Jesus demonstrated His love and forgiveness toward Peter. He told Mary who went to the tomb to anoint Him, to go tell

His disciples, and Peter, that He had risen. Peter was still one of the disciples, but Jesus knew that Peter needed to be told by Him that he still belonged to Jesus, so He sent him a special word of encouragement.

The boldness of Peter that we later read about in the book of Acts, began as a result of being in the upper room when Jesus sent the Holy Spirit to live in the hearts of the believers who were present.

BOLD FOR CHRIST

Peter received the infilling of the Holy Spirit's power and was empowered with boldness; and, as a result, he was now the mouthpiece for Jesus. The power of the Holy Spirit made him fearless as he stood up and defended Jesus.

A note of interest -- it was in the same place where Peter denied Jesus that he was also brought before the council to give an account of his actions. This time, however, when Peter was questioned, his response was entirely different. I have discovered that often the Holy Spirit will take you back to the place where you failed and where the devil thought he won in your life, so you can regain your ground and be victorious over him. The devil may think he has won and defeated you, but God will always have the last word and He will vindicate you. I believe the two young girls and the by-standers to whom the Bible records Peter previously denied Jesus, were able to witness him boldly speaking up for His Savior thus Peter was vindicated in every way over the enemy.

BOLD FOR CHRIST

Peter was bold, tenacious, fearless, and willing. When the Holy Spirit came into his heart he could not help but speak the precious name of Jesus. He had a case of the "I can't help it." Fire was shut up in his bones and it had to be released. Jesus wants you to also be bold and fearless for Him. The same fire, power, and passion He gave Peter and John is yours for the asking.

Receive His precious gift today!

4 | PRAISE IN TROUBLED TIMES

Many of you have discovered the keys for victory during troubled times. You have found that praise is a weapon that keeps the enemy from harassing you. You have also discovered that, when you praise, the trouble that seems insurmountable, melts away. In praise, you are focused on God who is your source of help; and as you praise Him, He descends and begins to do battle on your behalf.

Praise, coupled with worship, gives you a huge advantage in troubled times. The other disciples, Peter and John discovered this in their time of trouble. They found the solution to keep them pressing forward when trouble tried to stop them.

Then came one and told them, saying, 'Behold, the men whom ye put in prison are standing in the temple, and teaching the people." Then went the captain with the officers, and brought them without violence; for they feared the people, lest they should have been stoned. And when they had brought them, they set them before the council; and the high priest asked them, say--ing, "Did not we straitly command that ye should not teach in this name? And, behold, ye have filled Jerusalem with your doctrine, and intend to bring this man's blood upon us." Then Peter and the other apostles answered and said: "We ought to obey God rather than men."

Acts 5:25 – 29 (KJV)

As Peter and John continued to min-ister in the name of Jesus, although they were forbidden to do so by the high priest, they encountered trouble. They chose obedience to God rather than man and continued in the work God had assigned them to do. They were regularly brought up on charges but they praised God in the midst of the trouble, and remained in one accord with God, each other, and the people.

They were unified and it ensured that they reached heaven with their prayers, their praise, and their worship, which brought them their freedom.

As they continued their journey, Peter realized boldness was from God and it was necessary to fulfill the course of his destiny, so he petitioned God for more of it. He also asked God to perform additional signs, wonders, miracles, and healings. God showed up and powerfully demonstrated His presence and His power in their midst. He filled the believers with the power of the Holy Spirit; and, as a result, they became even bolder in spreading the gospel of the kingdom to all the people they met.

Before you encounter trouble, learn to praise God. When you find yourself in trouble, and as you praise God, He will come to your rescue. When trouble tries to overcome you, praise will lift you up and out and will also keep you steady and secure. God does not abandon you when you face troubled times, He is with you encouraging, supporting, and guiding you. Someone coined this phrase,

PRAISE IN TROUBLED TIMES

"Trouble don't last always." Trouble will not last in your life. It has to pass because God is a God of love, mercy, and grace; and He will not allow trouble to ultimately overtake the lives of His children. He has made us overcomers through Christ Jesus.

5 | UNITY OF BELIEVERS

When believers are unified, power is released! Boldness comes when a group of people stand together against tyranny. Unity brings about the blessings of the Lord. When Peter, John, and the believers were unified, they experienced God's presence in an abundant way.

"The God of our fathers raised up Jesus, whom ye slew and hanged on a tree. Him hath God exalted with his right hand to be a Prince and a Savior, for to give repentance to

Israel, and forgiveness of sins. And we are his witnesses of these things; and so is also the Holy Ghost, whom God hath given to them that obey Him." When they heard that, they were cut to the heart, and took counsel to slay them.

Acts 5:30-33 (KJV)

The word unity means oneness, to be combined to bring about greater wholeness, to be in harmony, in agreement, and to be in one accord in attitudes, opinions, and intentions.

UNITY OF BELIEVERS

During the decade of the early church, and after the Holy Spirit descended on the believers, they became unified. They became one, having one heart, and were knitted in their faith. As a result of their unity, they distributed all their possessions among each other to ensure that no one was left with unmet needs. Their unity brought a new measure of grace upon their lives. Everyone who had lands and houses sold them then brought the money and laid it at the disciples' feet, and the disciples distributed it to those who were in great need. The people in the book of Acts discovered that they became powerful when they were unified.

The Holy Spirit unifies us as believers and makes us one in Christ. As we become one with the Holy Spirit, we experience greater unity. This unity helps us to give freely of ourselves without holding back. We also clearly see the needs around us and are moved with compassion to provide help. As we become knitted together with the Holy Spirit, we become unified with other believers around the world so we can impact the nations for God. Our unity brings about the power needed to show the world how awesome our God is. Unity amongst believers helps to draw men, women, and children into the kingdom of God because we are going about our Father's business. You will discover God's business is for us to bring salvation to all the people in the world, to heal the sick, and to deliver and set people free by His great and mighty power.

Boldness in Christ

There is a song that clearly tells what it means to be bold in Christ. As you read these words, let them take root in your heart.

"I am not ashamed of the gospel, the gospel of Jesus Christ. I am not ashamed to be counted, but I am willing to give my life. You see, I am ready to be what He wants me to be, to give up the wrongs for the right. Oh, I am not ashamed of the gospel, oh, I am not ashamed of the gospel, oh, I am not ashamed of the gospel, the gospel of Jesus Christ."

It is my prayer, as you begin to walk in boldness, you will know that God is with you each step of the way on your journey just as He was with His disciples. When you invite the Holy Spirit into your heart, you will become as bold as a lion. As He empowers you, you will become a mouthpiece for God, and He will show His glory, His boldness, and His power through you. Step out in boldness and become the conqueror you were created to be.

PRAYER OF SALVATION

Jesus, I invite You to come into my heart, forgive me of my sins, cleanse me from all unrighteousness, and make Your home in me. You promise if I confess my sins You will be faithful to forgive me. I humbly confess them now and ask Your forgiveness and pardon. I invite You to make Your home securely in my heart from this day forward. Thank You for saving and changing me, in Jesus name I pray. Amen!

OTHER BOOKS
BY AUTHOR

Called and Chosen for Destiny

Flow Through Me Lord

Freedom In The Son

Overcoming Loneliness and Aloneness

Show Me How To Love

Time In Life's Waiting Room

Winning In The Battles Of Life

Workbook:

Called and Chosen for Destiny

JOANMURRAY**MINISTRIES**
CHANGED LIVES

Would you like Joan Murray to speak to your group or event? If so, contact Larry Davis at 623-337-8710 or email LDAVIS@INTERMEDIAPR.COM.

If you want to purchase bulk copies of Title or buy another book for a friend, get it now at www.IMPRBOOKS.COM.

If you have a book you would like to publish, contact Terry Whalin at Intermedia Publishing Group, Inc. at 623-337.8710 or email TWHALIN@INTERMEDIAPUB.COM.